FANTASTICALLY
GREAT WOMEN
WHO WORKED WONDERS

Kate Pankhurst

Follow your **fantastically**

great dreams with ...

ROSALIND
FRANKLIN

MARIA
SIBYLLA
MERIAN

KATIA
KRAFFT

KATHERINE
JOHNSON

DR
JAMES
BARRY

Madam
C. J. Walker

Elizabeth
Magie

JUNKO
TABEI

ANNETTE KELLERMAN

SOPHIE BLANCHARD

Lotte Reiniger

ROSA MAY BILLINGHURST

THE MATCHGIRLS

How did they work wonders to become so **magnificently amazing?**

The women in this book achieved ASTOUNDING things in their jobs whilst facing challenges along the way from death-defying blizzards to sending people into space and standing up for what is RIGHT. But one of the biggest challenges of all was the idea that a woman would not be good at a job, just because she was a WOMAN!

Follow these BIG DREAMERS and GO-GETTERS to find out how **anything is possible when you make the most of YOUR talents ...**

MARIA SIBYLLA MERIAN

Maria Merian grew up in Germany in the **1650s and 60s**. At the time women had few opportunities to work, study or travel. Maria loved collecting insects and could never have imagined the **exotic places** her **love** of these tiny creatures would take her.

Most people thought insects were **disgusting** and that they should be avoided. But Maria thought they were **intriguing**. She collected countless specimens and published books that recorded every detail of their **life cycle**.

Maria was particularly interested in the **mysterious transformation** of a caterpillar into a moth or butterfly (known as **METAMORPHOSIS**).

HER DISCOVERIES CREATED A BUZZ...

Maria recorded that adult BUTTERFLIES, like me, laid EGGS. Before that people thought we were born from MUD!

Eggs

Maria painted us on the specific plants we like to eat and live on. This showed that all living things are interconnected. Today this area of science is called ECOLOGY.

Maria was not allowed to use oil paints. Oil paintings were very valuable so only MEN could paint them!

THE WONDERFUL TRANSFORMATION OF CATERPILLARS AND THEIR PARTICULAR PLANT NOURISHMENT

1679-1683

THE NEW BOOK OF FLOWERS 1675

INSECTS OF SURINAME

Maria moved to **Amsterdam**. There she saw HUGE butterflies and **glittering beetles** brought back by explorers from the **New World** (the Americas). Maria longed to study these exotic insects in their natural habitat. In **1699**, after selling some of her art to raise funds, Maria made the long journey by sea to **Suriname** in South America to carry out research for a **new book** ...

Maria's research was published in **1705** and, for the first time, brought the WILD NATURE of **Suriname** to readers in Europe ...

I kept specimens in boxes. This strange LANTERNFLY made so much noise I was woken in the night by it!

Hisss!

More WILD wildlife! A spider that EATS BIRDS!

To show readers how WILD Suriname was I painted this pineapple plant covered in COCKROACHES.

Maria's pioneering work helped to **transform** people's understanding of the natural world. She showed how different species rely on each other for survival. Generations of scientists have studied her work since and many of the names she gave her new **discoveries** are still used by naturalists today.

Yummy!

ROSALIND FRANKLIN

Rosalind Franklin was a brilliant scientist. Her research helped to unravel the secrets of **DNA***. Sadly, during her lifetime Rosalind did not get the credit she deserved for her part in this **groundbreaking discovery**.

In the early 1950s, at a time when few women worked in the sciences, Rosalind got a job researching **DNA** at King's College London, UK. Rosalind knew that **sharing ideas** could lead to scientific breakthroughs.

The patterns the **X-rays** produced on photographic paper revealed clues about what **DNA** looked like and how it worked ...

*DNA is the substance in the cells of living things that gives instructions on how to grow and develop. It is sometimes called the 'BLUEPRINT FOR LIFE'.

DNA sample

At that time scientists had deduced that **DNA** existed but couldn't see it under a microscope. Rosalind was skilled in a special technique that fired a beam of **X-rays*** through **DNA** ...

*X-RAYS are a type of invisible radiation that can be used to create photographic images which see inside things, including DNA.

KATIA KRAFFT

Raging lava flows, toxic ash clouds and volcanic bombs were all in a day's work for French volcanologist Katia Krafft and her husband Maurice. Katia started her career after finishing her studies. It was a job so risky that she was one of only a handful of people, and one of the only women in the 1970s, willing to study fierce and fiery volcanoes.

'Volcanologist' wasn't a job Katia could just apply for. It was a job she carved out for herself by getting as close as possible to volcanoes that at any moment could go ...

BOOM!

Katia risked her life to gather awe-inspiring photos, film and scientific observations. Her work soon earned her a reputation as one of the world's leading (and most daring) volcanologists. Countries under threat from eruptions turned to Katia for advice on evacuating homes near to active volcanoes.

KATIA'S KNOWLEDGE ABOUT THE DESTRUCTIVE POWER OF VOLCANOES SAVED MANY LIVES

If a volcano ERUPTS it is sensible to run towards it to avoid VOLCANIC BOMBS!

KATIA

volcanic BOMB!

MAURICE

"They are so POWERFUL, so BEAUTIFUL, so you can just fall in LOVE with it."

Katia kept notes about her scientific discoveries. It was an extremely dangerous job and she had to be VERY careful.

In 1991 on Mount Unzen in Japan **disaster struck**. Tragically Katia and her husband were unable to escape a flow of hot ash and toxic gases that had unexpectedly changed direction.

Over her 20-year career, Katia witnessed forces of nature few humans had been able to get close to before. She turned the extraordinary footage and research she gathered into films and books. This work shocked, stunned and educated people about the SPECTACULAR power of volcanoes.

KATHERINE JOHNSON

There wasn't a calculation too complicated for the extraordinarily talented mathematician Katherine Johnson. She was a BRIGHT STAR but because of segregation Katherine had to fight to SHINE. (Segregation laws in the USA at that time stopped black people from having the same opportunities as white people.)

In the 1950s, Katherine got a job as a 'computer' at NASA. Computers as we know them today hadn't been developed yet so NASA employed lots of women to help male scientists with the maths needed to fly spacecraft. Women were rarely considered for these top jobs – especially black women like Katherine.

Nobody expected Katherine to play a vital part in the THE SPACE RACE*, but they hadn't done their maths properly!

"The idea of going into SPACE was NEW and DARING. There were no textbooks so we had to write them."

*THE SPACE RACE:
During the 1950s and 60s, the USA and the Soviet Union (now Russia) competed to be the first to explore space.

FOLLOW THE ARROWS TO SEE HOW KATHERINE HELPED PLOT NASA'S JOURNEY TO THE STARS ...

DR JAMES BARRY

MARGARET ANNE BULKLEY

EXTRAORDINARY

A BRILLIANT MIND

Dr James Barry had a **BIG** secret ... *Shhh, Dr James Barry was actually a woman disguised a male doctor.* Her name was Margaret Ann Bulkley and she was born in Ireland around 1795. At the time women were not allowed to study medicine no matter how clever or ambitious they were.

The idea that a woman might examine people's bodies or make decisions about health was **UNTHINKABLE**. Many women's only option was to marry well or risk not being able to support themselves. This was **NOT** the life that Margaret wanted ...

"Were I not a **GIRL** I'd be a **SOLDIER**?"

Margaret said this in a letter to her brother in 1808.

FRUSTRATED

AMBITIOUS

BRAVE

REMEDIES BY A FINE DOCTOR

I know what will sort out this PROBLEM.

COURAGEOUS STEPS

FIG 1: A BIG DECISION, A BIG SECRET

Margaret longed for the same **LIFE CHANCES** men had. With the help of trusted family and open-minded close friends, Margaret transformed herself. If a woman couldn't train as a doctor, then a man could ...

AMBITION SALTS

DR JAMES BARRY

Don't judge me by my APPEARANCE. I am old enough AND tall enough to become a doctor.

HOPEFUL

DETERMINED

CONFIDENT

HOW to be a DOCTOR

FIG 2: A NEW IDENTITY

In 1809, while still a teenager, James enrolled as a medical student at Edinburgh University in Scotland. James confidently convinced everyone that he was old enough to train and that he would make a very GOOD DOCTOR.

After my training I may have looked for countries where I had more chance of working as a female doctor. But plans changed and I continued to work for the British Army.

FIG 3: A SUCCESSFUL CAREER

In 1813, James joined the army as a qualified doctor. He worked around the world and was promoted to one of the highest medical ranks in the army. He was a HIGHLY SKILLED doctor, well known for:

1. Delivering a baby in one of the first ever caesarean sections.

mother and child survived.

DISAGREE with me and I'll challenge you to a DUEL!!

2. Being eccentric and outspoken.

3. Demanding the best care and diet for patients.

see that these patients recieve BETTER food!

It was only when James died in 1865 that his secret was revealed. The story caused a **SENSATION**. Nobody could believe a woman could have had such an **INCREDIBLE** medical career. (Or that nobody had guessed who James had once been.)

BE WHO YOU WANT TO BE TONIC

THE BRAVE HEART OF A DOCTOR

Madam C.

"I got my START by giving myself a START."

MADAM C.J. WALKER

was born Sarah Breedlove in Louisiana, USA in 1867. Before slavery was abolished in the USA in 1865, Sarah's parents had been forced to work as slaves. The family remained so poor that Sarah had to work as a farmhand during her childhood. Escaping poverty was very difficult for black women like Sarah and when she grew up it remained difficult to earn a good living.

These struggles only made Sarah more **determined** to change her situation ...

REFUSING TO BE WASHED UP ...

While working long hours as a **washerwoman** Sarah's hair began falling out. (At the time scalp problems caused by unhealthy working conditions were very common.) The solution Sarah found led to her being one of America's first black self-made MILLIONAIRES!

I found HAIR PRODUCTS to restore my hair and got a job as a sales agent at the company who made them. I realised I was a natural SALES PERSON. So-why not set up my own HAIR CARE BUSINESS?

MEET ENTREPRENEUR EXTRAORDINAIRE
J. Walker

BEFORE

AFTER

WONDERFUL HAIR GROWER — MADAM C. J. WALKER'S

WALKER'S GLOSSINE

MADAM C. J. WALKER'S VEGETABLE SHAMPOO — MADAM C. J. WALKER MANUFACTURING

MADAM C. J. WALKER'S TETTER SALVE — MADAM C. J. WALKER MANUFACTURING

ALL SHAMPOOED AND SET FOR SUCCESS ...

In 1906, Madam C. J. Walker's very own **WONDERFUL HAIR GROWER** was launched. Other black women could see that the product worked for Sarah, so they rushed to try it for themselves. Soon Sarah was able to add **more products** to her range.

I used CLEVER adverts that showed my products gave RESULTS!

I used my husband's initials as they sounded RELIABLE. 'Madam' was used to make customers think of LUXURY French products.

I was a SLEEK BUSINESS-WOMAN.

I knew that regular hair washing prevented scalp problems.

No more DANDRUFF!

We are HAIR CULTURISTS!

Our job is to GROW HAIR!

I can support my family.

Madam C. J. Walker's BEAUTY CULTURE SCHOOL

WALKER'S

Don't be AFRAID to SHINE!

GOING TO GREAT LENGTHS ...

In **1910**, Sarah had plans to open a large factory to keep up with demand. She trained up other black women as sales agents, giving them the **opportunity** to escape poorly paid jobs and to improve their own lives.

MOUNT EVEREST 8,848m

JUNKO TABEI

FOLLOW JUNKO'S INCREDIBLE JOURNEY TO THE TOP OF THE WORLD

Junko Tabei was born in Miharu, Japan, in **1939**. When she was a girl, she discovered a **love** for mountains. Step by (sometimes perilous) step this passion took Junko to some very high places and turned a daring pastime into her profession.

In the **1960s**, Junko joined a mountain climbing club to improve her skills. More and more Japanese women were enjoying **mountaineering** in their spare time but some people disapproved of this because they didn't think it was what a respectable woman should do. Rumours even spread that Junko only climbed because it was a way to find a husband.

These rumours didn't stop Junko. She was fit, strong and able to keep up with male climbers. She was **determined** to …

TREK HARDER!

Junko formed The **Ladies Climbing Club**. They wanted to travel to the Himalayas in Nepal – home of the world's highest and most **treacherous** mountains.

Nepal here we come!

TO THE TOP!

After a **heart-stopping** ascent, at 12:30pm on May 16th 1975 Junko became the **first woman** to reach the top of Mount Everest! The expedition took almost six months to complete. Junko's **incredible** achievement made headlines around the world but it took a while for people to accept that things were changing and a woman could be a housewife, a mother and a **professional mountaineer**.

"This willpower you cannot buy with money or be given by others, it rises FROM YOUR HEART."

Elizabeth Magie

In the early 1900s, in the USA, Elizabeth Magie invented a board game called The Landlord's Game.

The aim of the game was to encourage players to think about the **problems** caused when those **rich** enough to own land, property and companies **greedily** charged high rent and bills.

The game wasn't a runaway success but lots of people enjoyed playing it. In **1904**, Lizzie filed for a **patent**. This listed Lizzie as the **inventor** of The Landlord's Game. It was supposed to mean that nobody could steal her idea, but not everyone played by the rules ...

Play the game!

FOLLOW ME!

Elizabeth Magie

"Let me tell you there are no FAIRER-MINDED beings in the WORLD than CHILDREN."

In The Landlord's Game, players travelled round the board BUYING up property.

Players with more properties made MORE MONEY by charging opponents rent.

Those who had **lucky rolls** of the dice could **BANKRUPT** everyone else, demonstrating that the world works in very unfair ways.

The world needs to change!

We made MILLIONS!

...while the poor got POORER!

NO TRESPASSING

LAND OWNED BY THE RICH

But Monopoly wasn't about trying to make the world fairer. Instead players had to ...

A SHOCKING REVELATION!

Twenty-one years later, in **1935**, the large games company Parker Brothers started selling a new board game called **Monopoly**. It was so similar to *The Landlord's Game* that Lizzie quickly realised Monopoly's inventor, Charles Darrow, was trying to pass off many of her ideas as his own! Worse still, he had turned the game into something it was never meant to be ...

MONOPOLY WAS ALL MY IDEA!
(Well, I may have borrowed a few ideas from a game you've probably never heard of.)

Monopoly's recognisable playing pieces were added by Charles.

GASP!

BUY, BUY, **BUY!**

MAKE MORE AND MORE

MONEY!

And to take GREAT DELIGHT in BANKRUPTING other players!

THE GAME OF LIFE

Today few people have heard of Lizzie Magie, *The Landlord's Game* **or her vision for what players could learn from it. Lizzie was treated unfairly but she won the game when it came to** sticking to her beliefs. **The important questions she asked about** MONEY **and** POWER **are still relevant today.**

I am the real WINNER!

A DEAL IS STRUCK

When Parker Brothers realised Charles Darrow hadn't thought of the ideas on his own they offered Lizzie **$500** and promised to sell two other games which she had designed to teach about making the world a better place. Lizzie had never found a games company willing to sell her work before so she accepted. Unfortunately this didn't turn out to be a good deal ...

CHEATS!

GO TO JAIL!

STRIKING A LIGHT

THE MATCHGIRLS

FOR THE RIGHTS OF WORKERS

GET TO WORK!

DO AS I SAY!

In London, UK, during the 1880s, very poor women and girls worked at the Bryant and May match factory. They were trapped working in dreadful conditions for very little money, while all the factory owners earned huge profits.

A group of the matchgirls risked their jobs by BRAVELY speaking to women's rights campaigner, Annie Besant, about what it was really like to work in the factory. In JUNE 1888, Annie printed their shocking stories.

In 1882 factory bosses even unveiled this statue of the prime minister to try to make themselves look generous!

I have PHOSSY JAW! An illness caused by working so closely with a DANGEROUS chemical called white phosphorus.

We work 14-hour days, standing the whole time!

We are FORCED to pay fines for going to the toilet or being UNTIDY.

The public were HORRIFIED. Factory owners thought that if they denied everything nobody would listen to the matchgirls. This plan BACKFIRED!

ANNIE BESANT

GASP!

THE MATCHGIRLS WALKED OUT ON STRIKE!

The strike made headlines ...

THE STAR
MATCHGIRLS STAND TOGETHER!

THE TIMES
PUBLIC DONATE MONEY FOR THE MATCHGIRLS

EVENING STANDARD
FACTORY BOSSES FORCED TO LISTEN

The public are behind us!

Thanks to donations we won't starve.

People stopped buying BRYANT and MAY matches!

During the strike the matchgirls boldly marched to the Houses of Parliament to discuss their plight.

Perhaps something should be done!

Hmm.

It ain't fair!

We'll show 'em!

We WON'T work until things change.

After two weeks the factory realised they had no choice but to admit they had been unfair and to promise to change their ways.

Follow me and we'll make change happen!

VICTORY!

UNION OF WOMEN MATCHWORKERS

To ensure that the factory owners stuck to this, the matchgirls formed the largest union of women workers in the country at that time.

The matchgirls were considered so poor and unimportant that nobody recorded the names of the women who led the strike. Their brave actions BLAZED a trail for the right of all workers to work in safety and to be shown RESPECT and FAIRNESS.

IN HER TRICYCLE WHEELCHAIR SHE
ROSA MAY

Rosa May Billinghurst was born in London, UK, in 1875. After suffering from a disease called polio in her childhood she was left unable to walk. Rosa lived at a time when people with disabilities were often considered to be weak, and women to be less important than men. But Rosa REFUSED to be held back by such attitudes ...

In 1907 Rosa joined the WSPU (Women's Social and Political Union) to try and make a change. Members of the WSPU were called SUFFRAGETTES and they campaigned for a change in the law to allow women to VOTE.

They believed that for the country to be a fairer place for everyone to live in, then *everyone* should be allowed to have a say in how it was run. For seven years Rosa worked tirelessly to get VOTES FOR WOMEN ...

JUST TRY GETTING IN MY WAY!

"BETTER conditions must exist for hard-working lives!"

HOW ROSA PUSHED FOR PROGRESS ...

COR BLIMEY!

These suffragettes are nothing but TROUBLEMAKERS!

SHE MARCHED!
Rosa was known to use her wheelchair to **charge** at police who tried to get in the way of suffragettes marching in the name of VOTES FOR WOMEN!

VOT

WAS A FORCE FOR CHANGE, SUFFRAGETTE...
BILLINGHURST

SHE REMAINED DETERMINED!

On numerous occasions the police **tipped** Rosa out of her wheelchair leaving her stranded. When pictures of Rosa being mistreated appeared in newspapers many people were **shocked** and it helped to win public **sympathy** for the suffragette cause.

How unladylike.

I neither want or need sympathy. BUT I do want to support VOTES FOR WOMEN!

BEASTS!

VOTES FOR WOMEN

Pesky suffragettes!

SHE USED DEEDS, NOT WORDS!

In **1912** Rosa, along with fellow suffragettes, destroyed the contents of postboxes. They did this to draw attention to the suffragette cause.

Rosa was arrested many times for her disruptive deeds. On one occasion it took **four** police officers to carry Rosa and her chair to the police station past **crowds of cheering supporters!**

We DESTROYED over 5,000 LETTERS.

"They cannot take away my FREEDOM of spirit or my DETERMINATION to fight this good fight to the END."

WE WANT VOTES

GO ROSA

ES FOR WOMEN

WE SUPPORT YOU ROSA!

It's thanks to Rosa and her fellow **SUFFRAGETTES** that the law was eventually changed in 1918, allowing some women over the age of 30 to vote.

ANNETTE KELLERMAN
SHE MADE A SPLASH

In the early 1900s, Annette Kellerman became known as the 'AUSTRALIAN MERMAID'. She grew up in Sydney, Australia, and began swimming as a child to strengthen her legs after they were weakened by an illness called rickets.

At the time people thought it was more ladylike for women to 'bathe' rather than swim. But paddling wasn't for Annette who was most at home in the water. This led to a series of ASTONISHING career moves that were as strong as her swimming strokes ...

"Swimming is a PLEASURE and a BENEFIT, a clean, cool, BEAUTIFUL, cheap thing we all can ENJOY"

RIDE A WAVE OF WATERY WONDER WITH ANNETTE ...

ANNETTE THE FASHION DESIGNER

Annette refused to wear the baggy bathing suits of the day that made swimming impossible. A woman revealing her body shape was considered SHOCKING but Annette created her own tight-fitting swimsuit that allowed her to move freely in the water.

Swim with me!

To help other women enjoy swimming I began selling my swimwear designs.

ANNETTE THE CHAMPION SWIMMER

In her new swimming costume Annette was free to set new women's SWIMMING WORLD RECORDS!

ANNETTE THE STAGE STAR

Annette wowed audiences in theatres around the world with her BREATHTAKING aquatic stage act!

ANNETTE THE MOVIE STAR

Annette also SPLASHED on to the big screen starring in hugely successful silent movies about MERMAIDS and magical creatures. She wore elaborate costumes and carried out all her own daring diving stunts!

Annette's achievements INSPIRED a generation of women to discover the freedom of dipping their toes in the water and to explore what their AMAZING BODIES could do.

ANNETTE THE HEALTH EXPERT

In 1918, Annette began writing books that showed women how to keep HEALTHY by being active. Encouraging women to take care of and be PROUD of their bodies was a very FORWARD-THINKING idea for the time.

Lotte Reiniger

Once upon a time, there was a German girl who was fascinated by fairy stories. Her name was Lotte Reiniger ...

Growing up in the early 1900s Lotte loved to build traditional shadow puppet theatres. All she needed to create **MESMERISING** fairy tale worlds was paper, scissors and the **DAZZLING** magic of her imagination. Lotte grew up to become one of the world's first and most important animators ...

While working on a film set in 1918 Lotte's **TALENT** was spotted. She was asked to animate wooden rats because real rats could not be trained to do as the director wished!

Lotte went on to make lots of short animated films based on the traditional tales and shadow puppet theatres she found so MAGICAL ...

"I just want to tell STORIES, spin a yarn, DREAM"

Each animation had THOUSANDS of frames!

SNIP! SNIP! SNIP!

Lotte animated our bodies to show how we felt.

Lotte moved us slightly between frames.

The film took 3 years to make.

While working on her film Lotte invented the 'MULTI-PLANE CAMERA'. It was a huge technological breakthrough as for the first time an animation had 'DEPTH'.

HOW IT WORKED ...

In 1923, Lotte began work on the oldest surviving feature length animated film, THE ADVENTURES OF PRINCE ACHMED ...

The multi-plane camera filmed objects at different distances from the camera.

I am close to the camera, so I look near!

I am in the background so I look FAR AWAY!

Eleven years later, the famous American animator WALT DISNEY adapted the multi-plane camera to make Snow White and the Seven Dwarfs. Many people wrongly thought that Disney developed the multi-plane camera on his own and that his film was the first animated feature film.

During her long career Lotte ended up making over 40 animated films and working into her 80s.

Lotte worked at a time when few women had jobs in the film industry but her films were too magical to remain in the shadows.

The End.

MEET RISING SENSATION SOPHIE BLANCHARD

In Paris, France, in 1809 Sophie Blanchard's husband (a HOT-AIR BALLOON showman) died and Sophie was left to pay his large debts. At that time it was difficult for a woman to find a well-paid job. Even though she was shy and nervous Sophie decided that the only way out of her desperate situation was to take over her husband's business, making her the FIRST PROFESSIONAL FEMALE AERONAUT. Crowds FLOCKED to witness not only a hot-air balloon, but one with a WOMAN piloting it...

By making SMART DECISIONS, like using less fuel by flying in a smaller balloon, Sophie managed to pay off her debts and made a GOOD LIVING for herself.

UP!

flying is a 'SENSATION INCOMPARABLE' (A sensation unlike anything else).

C'est magnifique!

Sacré bleu!

Sophie's shows were SO popular that she became the official AERONAUT of the French emperor and, later, French royalty.

AND AWAY! UP!

I WOWED audiences by flying in SMALLER and SMALLER baskets...

Oh la la!

Mon Dieu!

THE RISKY BUSINESS OF BALLOONING ...

To make her shows even more SPECTACULAR, Sophie threw FIREWORKS over the side of her balloon. (This was VERY DANGEROUS as the hydrogen gas used to inflate her balloon was extremely flammable.) More than once Sophie accidentally flew so high that she passed out due to lack of oxygen and on one flight the weather became so cold that ICICLES formed on her hands and face!

Sadly Sophie's EXTRAORDINARY career ended tragically. In 1819, fireworks ignited Sophie's balloon and she was unable to control its descent.

Her REMARKABLE and ADVENTUROUS spirit was remembered by the people of Paris with a special balloon shaped memorial inscribed with the words 'Victim of her own art and intrepidy'.

FANTASTICALLY GREAT WORDS

Aeronaut someone who pilots an airship or hot-air balloon

Altitude measures how far away from the Earth's surface you are

Altitude sickness causes headaches, loss of appetite and trouble sleeping when you can't get enough oxygen from the air at high altitudes

Avalanche a sudden rush of a large amount of snow down a mountainside

Bankrupt when someone has no money left

Career the work someone does for a long period of time

Caesarean section when a baby is born by surgery

Disability a mental or physical difference that can sometimes make it difficult for a person to walk, see, hear, speak or do other activities

Disguise to pretend to be someone or something else

Entrepreneur a person who creates a business

Environment the air, earth, water, plants and animals that surround us

Evacuate to remove people from danger

Exotic from another country

Flammable something that catches fire easily and quickly

Life cycle the entire life of an animal, plant or human from birth to death

NASA stands for National Aeronautics and Space Administration and the people who work here study the outer space

Nobel Prize a special award given to new people every year who have done extraordinary things for the world

Oxygen an element in the air that is necessary for life

Phossy jaw a disease that affected people who worked closely with a chemical called white phosphorus which destroys the bones of the jaw

Polio a disease which causes very weak muscles that can make it difficult for some people to move

Rickets a condition that results in weak or soft bones

Strike when people purposely stop going to work to try to make changes

Specimen a single animal or plant that represents an entire species

Soviet Union a country that existed from 1922 to 1991, made up of Russia and many other states that are now separate countries

Suffragette a woman who campaigned for women to be allowed to vote

Union a group of workers who join together to protect the rights of other members

Volcanologist a scientist who studies volcanoes